Prayer Bundle

by Toon Hermans

**translation by
John F. Jansen in de Wal**

Sheed & Ward

Sheed & Ward™ is a service of National Catholic Reporter Publishing Company, Inc.

ISBN: 1-55612-459-7

Published by: Sheed & Ward
115 E. Armour Blvd. P.O. Box 419492
Kansas City, MO 64141-6492

To order, call: (800) 333-7373

Contents

Note from the Translator

Toon Hermans is one of the greats in Dutch Cabaret. Behind the smile, the quip, the song and dance of the public man lies the pain of private suffering. But for his faith he would have succumbed and long since disappeared from the stage.

The simple dimensions of his faith, a faith tested in the crucible of life, sustained his and then my life. To share with you this sustenance is my purpose in this translation.

May you gain strength and courage from Toon's reflections on Jesus of Nazareth, and trust enough to say, "Look my way."

This is my prayer for you.

Lord, hear my prayer.

❖ Union ❖

Lord,
praying doesn't always work
no matter how well intentioned I am.
But when it works,
the circle closes
and I feel deep inside me
the fullness that exists
between You and me.

❖ Praying ❖

Praying means:
react to the love
that God gives us.
To love the man from Nazareth
to really love Him
that is praying.
Rejoicing in the stable of Bethlehem
to be touched under the Cross of Golgotha
to long for Him,
hope in him
trust in him
every moment of the day;
that is praying.

❖ Breath ❖

Praying is the breath
of my soul
fanning the fire
in my heart;
is the warmth
in my life.

❖ Consolation ❖

Lord,
not a leaf falls from a tree
except for You.
You are present in all life
and in the course of events.
You know of my joys
my trials
and of my tears.
Let that thought
give me consolation.
You lift up what has fallen
and make it new.

❖ Secrets ❖

Lord,
I have no answer
to your miracles.
Thinking or knowing
do not help me even one bit.
Your secrets
are unfathomable
but your love
is clear as water.

❖ Prayer of the Day ❖

Lord,
in the morning
I ask for your blessing.
Maybe I do that
because I like to live.
Always I hope anew
that You will bless my days.
Yes, I love life
and fill the glass to the brim,
but I know for certain, Lord,
that I will find
this life meaningless
as of the day
that I can hope no more
in You.

❖ Trust ❖

Lord,
I do not know
what tomorrow will bring.
Nor do I know
what comes after this life.

Those who know your love
blindly trust
in your purposes.

Give me that trust, Lord.

*   *   *

When I
stand at the deathbed of another
I always feel the lesser.

❖ Lindeboom ❖

I once wrote the preface to the volume of verse "Now I want to Sleep and Forget" 1984, by Ben Lindeboom. The author had been my children's doctor. I had not seen him in years, but when he was seriously ill and had only a short while to live, he telephoned me. Never before had I heard anyone speak with such composure and surrender about his final phase in life. He said that he didn't believe in anything, yet. In his volume I found this prayer:

Oh, God, in whom I don't believe,
I call upon you, for I have no one
who can help me now.

My friends and companions I asked,
Pray for me, that my luck may change yet.
Still, what is done is done.
But Great God, in whom I believe,
I'm in such pain, I do hurt so.

The sign of a man
who in his utter helplessness
seeks God. A prayer that, more than
containing a rejection of the thought of God
is a humble apology.

❖ The Other ❖

Lord,
give me the grace
to see my fellow man
with eyes of love.
Make me humble
and unselfish
for only in that way
will I reach
others
who need my love.

❖ At the Center ❖

Lord,

inspire me.

Let me place you at the center of

my life

in my home and in my work

and that I do so

as a matter of fact.

You are no distant God

on a high cloud

but an everyday God

who lives in all people.

Let me invite you

into the city

and celebrate You

as the man from Nazareth

amid a multitude

and then I hope

that for a moment

You'll look my way.

❖ Courage ❖

Lord,

I am not worthy

to speak with You

but when I reflect on your holy suffering

and consider what you have done for us

then I take heart

and say again,

"Lord, hear my prayer."

❖ The Truth ❖

Lord,
at times I'm ludicrous
tragi-comic
for then I live
so self-assured
next to the truth.
Open my eyes.
You are
The Way, The Truth
and the Life.

❖ Breath ❖

Lord,
I am not life.
Life lives in me
but it is Your breath
not mine.
I only breathe Your breath
in and out.
Let me
reflect on this each day
so as to thank You
in that thought.

❖ Who Am I? ❖

Lord,
I pray
often out of fear
and sometimes still
of gratitude.
Yet, I have for the second
more reason
than the first.
Who am I, by myself?
What I am
comes from You.

❖ Years ❖

I have at times asked myself,
am I here only
to a specific day
a specific hour
and does it all then end abruptly?
I have at times thought that.
Yes, a thought without prospect.
When I close my eyes
does everything end?
Was that handful of years
the whole purpose of my existence?
When you reflect more deeply
you suddenly feel
that there is more;
that the God of heaven and earth
has other purposes
for his dearest
and most beloved creation
than but few years on earth
where there is nearly always
discord and disharmony.

❖ Salvation ❖

Lord,
how many times haven't You
saved me already?
Again and again
You helped me up
and gave me strength
when I was disheartened.
You gave me light in darkness.
When I had to say farewell
to people dear to me
You were my comfort.
Thus You have become
a part of my life.
Stay with me, Lord,
in all I do.
Without You
I won't make it.

❖ Solemn ❖

When in my smallness I turn to God,
I look up to something indescribably
majestic.
Yet, in Jesus' passionate love
I can hardly find anything solemn.

❖ The Everyday ❖

Lord,
I pray, let me meet You
in ordinary everyday human things;
in a handshake and a smile
in a caress or a tear
in the little things around me
and in every moment of the day.

❖ Courage ❖

Lord,
give me the courage
to accept
that you hear me
so that I'll continue
to always anew
ask You for help.

❖ Everywhere ❖

There are people who, when they pray, feel
closely bound to God.

Then there are people who, always and everywhere,
carry that same feeling with them. They have as it
were,

become prayer.

❖ Peace ❖

Lord,

hear me

and my colorless prayer will become

living language.

Many times You have

greeted your friends

with the words 'Peace be with you.'

Please say it even once to me

and never again shall I fear.

With Your peace in my heart

I will not be troubled.

❖ Love ❖

Lord,
You are love itself.
You taught us
to love one another.
But we fight each other,
we envy one another.
Maybe we're on our way
to self-destruction.
Where is love?
Isn't it a match anymore for chaos
hate and enmity?
Lord, give us love
come to our aid
we do not know what we do.

❖ Light ❖

Lord,

when darkness comes to my heart

give me

the light of Bethlehem.

❖ When I Know ❖

When I know
that there is an almighty God
who loves me
and who has mercy on me,
how then can I be troubled
or uneasy.

❖ Blessing ❖

There are people, Lord,
who feel guided by You
from morn to eve
from dusk to dawn
all of their lives.
They have been blessed with a great and deep
faith;
a blessing
for which I can
endlessly long.

❖ Ego ❖

Lord,
I often pretend.
I exaggerate.
That's when I want to
assert my influence.
In your presence all that is meaningless
for You see through
my pitiful ego.
Give me that prayer
of perfect sincerity.

❖ Temptation ❖

Lord,
I would like to be an angel
but I am a man.
I cannot resist the temptation
and each time anew I hope for forgiveness.

❖ Sun ❖

Lord,
it is no exaggeration
when at times we call this earth
a valley of tears.
Yet, You create within that self-same earth
much innate joy.
There is so much mirth
in the sunny hues
of trees, plants and flowers
and the joy in us
also comes from You.
Place a joyful prayer
on my lips, Lord
a song
a melody of gratitude
rapturous words
about all the good in this life.
Teach me to pray
when the skies darken, Lord,
but accept my joy too as a
prayer.

❖ Night ❖

Lord,
it is night
it is dark
it is still
and I'm alone,
but when I speak
softly with You
the dark is a different dark
the stillness a different stillness
the night a different night
and I am different when alone.
Fill my heart, Lord,
with Your mercy
and bless these hours.

❖ Light ❖

Lord,
as the light
breaks through the night
and spreads
and touches all things
so Your love for me breaks through
the darkest days.
Give me the strength
to catch
the warm light of your love
and the day will be blessed.

❖ Father ❖

Father in heaven,
I call upon You
when it goes badly with me.
When there is hardly any prospect
You often bring a great conversion.
Jesus too did that.
In the Garden of Gethsemany he felt fear
and called upon the Father in Heaven.
I beseech You, together with Jesus
let me also call upon You as Father
when things go well with me.

❖ Weak ❖

Lord,
I am weak
and repeatedly break down
in the same faults.
I want to become stronger
and better.
That is possible only
if You help me.
Hear me, Lord,
and stand by me.

❖ Making Contact ❖

Lord,

that You are interested

in each of us individually

is hard to imagine.

But, once in a while

I feel IT'S SO.

Then a deep peace

engulfs me.

❖ Let us Pray ❖

Lord,
I pray
let me pray
give me the right words
to come nearer to You.
Give me the courage
to openly and honestly
and from within
speak with You.
Let me then feel the warmth
of a prayer.

❖ Meeting ❖

Lord,
I'm easily jealous of
the fishermen of Galilee
who sat with You
in a fishing boat.
I would like that too
and how happy I would be,
happy as a child,
to be allowed so close to You.

❖ Spring ❖

Lord,
let me look up
at the cross,
and when I can't go on
lay down
my prayer
like fresh flowers
at your crucified
feet.

Be the spring
from which I draw
when the river
of my life
has dried up.

❖ Suffering ❖

There is no cry so full of loneliness and
helplessness as the cry of Jesus in his
death throes.
"My God, My God, why have You forsaken me."
This lamentation clearly shows that,
to the bitter end, he desired to be the paragon
of all human suffering;
that he sacrificed
himself for us and desired to precede us through
earthly suffering to a glorious resurrection.

❖ Suffering ❖

Lord,
when I suffer
bring me Your holy suffering
in remembrance.
It'll strengthen and encourage me.
I pray,
ask the Father in heaven
to hear me then
and to have mercy on me.

❖ To Profess ❖

Lord,
when I profess with my lips
that I steadfastly trust in You
let it be the full truth.
As the sponge fills itself with water
so fill my heart
with unhesitating trust
in Your goodness and mercy.

❖ The Light ❖

Lord,
when I was in the deep valley
and there wasn't a speck to be seen
of the light at the top,
I called upon you
and it became lighter.
The light came into the valley
and along its beam
I climbed up again,
laboriously,
but once at the top
I saw the light
in its fully glory.
My suffering was over
and thankfully
I embraced your light.
Now I am certain:
you are the radiant light
at the top of the mountain
but also
the glimmer of the spark in the valley.

❖ Human ❖

For centuries people have expostulated
how they must live.
But the great, shining example is Jesus.
The Son of God become man.
Whosoever contemplates on His unselfish love
must be convinced that no one can help us
to become HUMAN more than He.

❖ I Would Like to Know ❖

Lord,
there are people who celebrate you
in mighty cathedrals
and robed in purple vestments.
There are those also who call upon you
wrapped in rags
filthy and hungry
lying along the side of the road.
I would like to know, Lord,
to whom your ear
is inclined to listen most.

❖ Blessing ❖

Lord,

here in this silent landscape

in the silence of the open field

it is as if, in the noon light,

I can perceive some of your glory.

I thank you

for this stirring.

I take it

as a blessing.

❖ Wonder ❖

Lord,

technological developments wash over me

as an unstemmable tidal wave.

Perplexing electronic gadgets

become the common property of society.

Lord, help me understand

that all these are only

small fabrications

and that one bird

that rises into the clouds

carries more wonder within

than all the wonders of technology

together.

❖ Our Father ❖

Lord,
I pray to you as Our Father
give me the courage
to entrust to you
in the ways of a child
everything and anything.

Into my heart
pour that childlike sense
that enables me
to experience you
in my prayers
as my Father.

❖ Children ❖

When we think upon the eternal God and His secrets,

we need no more understanding than a child.

All that we have as excess spiritual baggage

doesn't bring us a step closer, but increases the chances for confusion.

Listen to the purity of speech of children.

Before God too they clearly say what it's all about.

❖ Solemnities ❖

Lord,
you are so infinitely great
the solemnities we think up
to celebrate you
fall short.
How are we
in our insignificance to praise you
to pay homage?
It won't do.
It seems as if external display
does not reach you.

Ceremonies are, in word and form
often so bombastic
so earthly.
Between you and me
only inner communication
is possible.
I succeed more by coming to you
with nothing more than my suffering
because you are, above all, the God of love
and mercy.

❖ Beside Me ❖

Lord,

I know not where you are

where you live in all this

but when everything became very difficult

I suddenly knew

You stood beside me.

I could talk with you.

I did that then.

It gave relief.

Thank you, Lord,

I now know that I can count on you.

❖ Questions ❖

In our most fervent prayers we promise
to follow you, Lord,
and to remain true to your commands.
During your life on earth
your own friends
deserted you.
"I don't know that man."
Lord, what are your plans for me?
How do you enable me
to withstand the worldly
and to grow beyond it?
Is it my weakness that touches you?

❖ I Remember ❖

I remember my own failed prayers.

I remember melancholy prayers, heavily laden and sentimental.

I remember flattering prayers, unreal and bethought.

I remember arrogant prayers.

But along with the dramatic prayers in moments that offered hardly any prospect, I also remember the joyful prayers, the glad-to-be-alone prayers, that, without exaggeration, I may call the dance-prayers. For often I have thanked the God in heaven for the fantastic days and then I couldn't contain my body; it danced and the dance was my prayer.

I then felt an authenticity tremble through my bones: the joy of life. Actually that is my dearest prayer. Stronger than silent meditation or the light lispel in a pew.

When the whole body gets involved in prayer and dances to gratitude in the Creator, unrehearsed, pure, from the bottom of the heart . . .

Lord, bless us with such blissful moments, let us dance in joyful prayer.

❖ "It" ❖

'How-goes-it . . .'
'I-know-it . . .'
"It" *is a much-encompassing word.*

Lord,
you are *it*
the endless *it*
the unspeakable *it*
the all-encompassing *it*.
All else is incomparable.

❖ The Other ❖

Lord,
who would I search
for myself
if I have not first
found the other.
Grant that I recognize
the other in myself
for every man
is created
in your image and likeness.

❖ The Day ❖

We fill the days of our lives by doing all kinds
of things. That is allright, but we have to
guard against losing sight of the day itself.
The day is a gift. First comes the gift, and
only then you see what you can do with it.

❖ Mystery ❖

Lord,
what am I to do?
The mystery of an eternal God
is beyond me.
I can't say a meaningful word
about it.
But then, who can?
I cling
to the man of Nazareth
who in His selfless love
by His word
by His life
and by His suffering for us
to the intentions of an eternal God
gave substance.

❖ Seasons ❖

And when the new light came
the new light came to me
and when the new green came
the new green came to me
and when the new sun came and smiled
the new sun smiled in me.
Thus it had to be
the dark, the pain, the sorrow
the loneliness; they lay behind me
when the new light came.
You can't summon it
or light it up
it comes when it wills.
Leave it be
let come over you
for all comes from His hands.

❖ Miracle ❖

Lord,
it's not the smile of the child
not the color of the flower
that touch me.
The real touch
comes from the invisible miracle of creation
which is hidden
in all that lives.
Touch me, Lord,
with that emotion
and teach me
to be
a meaningful part
of all you have created.

❖ Soul ❖

Lord,
you made of us
the most consequential creature
on this earth
for within us you created a soul.
We cannot point it out
as we point out our limbs
and our brain
with which we think.
But by your grace we feel
that we live from the Soul
and that the power
of its immateriality
supersedes by far
that of the materiality.

❖ Stillness ❖

Lord,
I close my eyes
there's momentary stillness.
I try to think of you
wait for a moment
to see if a little spark
of your love
will kindle in me.
And when you bless my thoughts
I feel you near
and the stillness
touches me propitiously.

❖ Ten Commandments ❖

Lord,

see what has become

of this world

give me anew

your Ten Commandments

and the strength to do

in all simplicity

what, in them, you hold before us.

❖ Search ❖

Newspapers and magazines are full of what we need to do to live healthy lives, to become more fit than we are and to postpone aging.

Spiritual life is hardly mentioned.

When at times I turn into myself to search for who I really am, and I find only myself, I am disappointed.

I desire to find within myself something of the Creator who created me, for in His light I see myself more completely.

To be myself through Him, that's what I ask in prayer.

❖ Balance ❖

Lord,
thinking of you
and contemplating your simplicity
I pray
curb my desire to impress
and my striving for distinction.
Give me peace of heart
the balance
between myself and others.

❖ At Times ❖

Lord,

at times it is as if you don't exist.

Then all is empty

lonely and cold.

But when again

I feel your mercy

a warmth surrounds my heart

as from a fire

and I turn anew

to you

with hopeful heart.

❖ To Believe ❖

Everyone can, aside from thought
in all that lives
awaken to a power
that is not of this world
that does not come from man
but from a higher plane.
Whoever perceives the mystery hidden in life
comes to God
and is a believer.

❖ To Look ❖

Look at man
and see the wonder within.
You see it not
then look again
and again
and again
and when you look well
you can see the wonder within.
It moves
it speaks
it listens
it laughs
it touches you
and speaks of love.
Something as great as man
has to be destined
for something other, a higher plane
than life on earth.
Look at man
and see the wonder.

❖ Belief ❖

I believe in the great men and women
who preceded us into eternity
and whom we call saints.
I have a few who accompany me
on my life's journey.
A relic of St. Gemma
I cherish as a valuable gem.
She was a simple nun from Lucca
Italy.
Not a day or a night do I live without her.
Always again I ask her anew,
"Saint Gemma, so close to Jesus, hear our
prayer."

❖ Temptation ❖

Lord,
the world comes at me
with its temptations
like a blossoming apple tree.
I am no stronger than Adam.
He couldn't withstand the temptation.
Neither can I.
Every day again
we lose paradise.
It is in us
to taste
the forbidden fruits.
Thanks be to God
that you are
full of forgiveness.

❖ To Save ❖

Lord,
I do not know
I do not know
that is my prayer.
I search for you
but I do not know where
I can find you.

In the appearance of bread and wine . . .

But I want to see you more clearly
I want you close to me
and not let go
not for anything in the world.
I don't believe I'll ever make it.

I am too weak for it.
Always there is the world
that distracts me from your love.
Have mercy on me.

❖ Childlike ❖

Not long ago I heard a world famous artist, who may be called a giant, both spiritually and physically, say these words, 'I'll light a candle for you, before Mary!' I'll not ever forget the childlike way in which he said it.

It is the appropriate manner.

It is THE manner by which to gain favor with Mary.

She the Mother, we the children.

❖ Imagine ❖

When you know someone loves you
forgives you all
stands by you always
never lets you fall
because he knows your weakness
that is a tremendous feeling.
Now imagine
that that someone is
the God of heaven and earth.

❖ Mary ❖

During the month of May, the rosary was said at our house. I was still a child. May was Mary's month. We picked flowers in the field and placed them before the blue-white statuette of Mary that stood in a corner of the room, on a small table, on which lay a lace coverlet. The rosary has, in our time, become an item very seldom seen. It's been made into a sort of ring with a mere ten beads on it. Not bad, but the old one was more beautiful.

To be honest, I thought the old one somewhat lengthy. Maybe that's because of the coco-nut mat. In the evening we lit the little votive light that stood before the statue of Mary and then, kneeling, we said the rosary. I used to kneel in my bare knees on a coarse, red coco-nut mat, and that was a feeling that, while I describe it, I can feel all over again. But what it was all about, was Mary.

My mother led in prayer and we, three brothers and I, responded. That was not a special devotion in our family. In the street where we lived it was done in just about every house.

When that plain room comes back to mind, it's as if I can hear the voices from afar. I walk again in the fields to pick flowers and I see a flickering votive light, just like then.

Mary was part of the family. Along with our own mother you had another mother, a mother full of grace. As a child you didn't know exactly what grace was, but you knew that it had something to do with love between this mother in heaven and the children on earth.

Now I understand that there is not a more chosen person than the mother of Jesus of Nazareth. I lost sight of her for a long time, but she is now back in my heart and I feel stronger and safer. Sometimes she gives me back that warm feeling of that room with the flickering votive light. Through the centuries great artists have portrayed her with purple mantles and with golden crowns on her head. The mysterious part is that, no matter how highly exalted we may consider her, through that loftiness radiates simplicity, the humble love of a mother who is approachable for all and who cares. For she is a consoling mother, a helping, a giving mother. A mother in the true sense of the word.

❖ Prayer ❖

Mother Mary, my own mother told me about you
when I was a child. Since then I have known who
you are. I know you are a fountain of grace,
and that you have heard million of people who
have called upon you.
When I look at your image, a warmth goes out
from it as if to say. 'Tell me what's on
you mind and I'll help you'. Not without
reason are you called Mother of Perpetual Help.
Help us Mary, day in and day out,
always and everywhere, do not desert us.

❖ Mary ❖

Mary,
all over the world
people call upon you.
You are honored and lauded
in all tongues.
You have been praised
in a multitude of titles,
but whether you are called
Ivory Tower or House of Gold
before all you are Mother.
Mother Mary, give me the strength
to see you as my mother.
Come under my roof
into my house.
In all I do, let me
first deliberate with you
and make me think of
what you have suffered under the cross
of Golgotha, where your Son
hung dying.

❖ Surrender ❖

Lord,
we believe that you are Lord
over life and death.
That thought gives us hope.
But when we lose someone
who is dear to us
we have no answer.
Lord,
let us lay our lives
in your hands,
and teach us to say
over and over,
'Your will be done'.

❖ Candle ❖

I don't know how may people wrote to me
—when things went badly with me—'We'll light
a candle for you'.
People from all walks of life, among them
purified people who once had to fight hard.
In such a moment you feel that such a
candle flame is not just a sentimental light.
When one takes a candle and a match and
lights that candle for another, there really is
warmth in the one for the other. Thousands
upon thousands of people light a candle
every day. That is quite different than
when thousands of people do not light a
candle.
Praying is not just 'asking for yourself,'
but it is also asking for the other. Just
as when you light a candle for another, so
a connection is established among people in
prayer, and that is a great power in the
community of man.